Bury My Heart In Birmingham, the Lamar Weaver Story

Bury My Heart In Birmingham, the Lamar Weaver Story

Warriors Of The Civil Rights Movement

Reverend Lamar Weaver
and Rueben Jackson

Edited by
Dolores Ann Jackson

Writers Club Press
San Jose New York Lincoln Shanghai

Bury My Heart In Birmingham, the Lamar Weaver Story
Warriors Of The Civil Rights Movement

Writers Club Press
an imprint of iUniverse.com, Inc.

For information address:
iUniverse.com, Inc.
5220 S 16th, Ste. 200
Lincoln, NE 68512
www.iuniverse.com

ISBN: 0-595-18749-8

Printed in the United States of America

To the memory of our mothers, Mrs. Ruby Aileen Harris Weaver and Mrs. Victoria Rogers Jackson

Epigraph

We are caught in an inescapable network of mutuality, tied in a single garment of destiny. What ever affects one directly, affects all indirectly.

Martin Luther King, Jr.

Contents

Preface

I had the pleasure and honor of meeting Lamar Weaver by a strange coincidence. A friend of mine and I were having an interesting discussion about the current state of affairs of Blacks in politics, Black people in general and other related matters. Rev. Weaver was standing nearby and overheard a portion of the discussion. At some point in the discussion. he said "amen brother", and from that rather inauspicious encounter a great friendship was born.

To say that Lamar Weaver is a man of great courage would be an understatement. It would be like saying Mahatma Ghandi was just a shop steward, or that Dr. Martin Luther King, Jr. was just another good speaker. Before you decide that this man or any other person you have never heard of is even worthy of being mentioned in the same sentence as Ghandi or King let me qualify my statement. The courage and leadership that Ghandi and King demonstrated arose as a result of the great injustices that their respective cultures experienced during that period of history. They were responding as victims of injustice in the self-interest of their own respective cultures. It was the collective suffering of their own people that gave rise to their taking a stand and fighting back. It can be argued that it is inevitable

that you can suppress the human spirit for only so long
before it will rise up in rebellion. That is only natural.
You can beat a dog only so much before it will turn and
bite you. However, there is a different kind of courage
that is rarely demonstrated by ordinary men. That kind
of courage is unselfish courage. Unselfish courage is the
courage to do things that take you out of your comfort
zone. How much courage does it really take to motivate
someone to want to come out of a fire to save themselves? On the other hand it takes extraordinary
courage to *go into* a fire to save another without regard
for your own safety. This kind of courage is the most
God-like. I believe that men can only be inspired by
God to have this kind of courage. And like so many of
the other great gifts that God has given mankind, it
often goes unrecognized and unappreciated.

This book is the story of one such example of great
unselfish courage. It is also the story of the extraordinary courage of many people both Black and White,
who were the unsung heroes of the Civil Rights
Movement. These were the people who remained
behind to suffer in small towns and cities across the
south after the flames of hatred were fanned by the
activities of the Civil Rights leaders. Many of these
unsung heroes were considered troublemakers and rab-
ble-rousers by their family, friends and neighbors. In
many places, the freedom riders were not welcomed by
the citizens they were there to help because there would
be hell to pay after the freedom riders left town. The
real heroes of the Movement are the hundreds of Black

and White people who risked their lives and, in some cases, even lost their lives. They made great sacrifices of their families, reputations and ways of life for the principle of justice and equality.

The Civil Rights Museum located in Birmingham, Alabama has an impressive collection of images and historical artifacts. It probably has the most complete collection of historical pieces housed under one roof. Unfortunately, it too is incomplete. There is very little information on the contribution of the White, Jewish and Italian people who made significant contributions to the Civil Rights effort. Without the help and sympathy of many of the most powerful and influential Whites, Jews and Italians, change would not have taken place. Who is to say how many attitudes of everyday Whites were changed in Las Vegas by Frank Sinatra's insistence that Sammy Davis Jr., be treated fairly? Virtually all of the elected officials who were instrumental in drafting legislation ending segregation were White. All of the Supreme Court Justices and all of the Federal Court judges who were courageous enough to do what was right, were White. These people had the courage to make decisions that were based on principle and not what was politically correct for that day. It is easy to miss this most important point until you recognize how difficult it is today to not conform to what is politically correct. Today no political or even religious public figure would dare criticize the homosexual life style without instant backlash and even character assassination. Entire careers can be ruined and people may face loss of jobs for merely making a politically incorrect statement. The late Jimmy the Greek and Anita Bryant are just two such persons whose entire careers were ruined because of what they said. The backlash that non-Blacks faced for their support of the Civil Rights Movement was even greater in those days because they could actually lose their lives as many Whites and Jews did. Obviously, the many millions of Blacks who were the target of the horrors of slavery, hatred and racism ultimately suffered the most. However, I believe that if there is ever to be any real healing and progress in race and ultimately human relations we must unite based on our commonalties and not our differences. The Whites, Jews, Italians and other non-Blacks who had the courage to join Blacks during the most difficult period of the Civil Rights Movement did so because of a recognition of the commonalties between all men. This is a fact that should never be overlooked, forgotten or unappreciated. Just as Black people resent being stereotyped as lazy, ignorant and predisposed to criminal behavior because of the actions of a few Blacks, White people who are not racists and hate mongers probably resent being judged by the actions of those Whites who are. The Civil Rights Movement has never been a battle between Black and White-it is a battle between right and wrong. This is the essence of what I believe that Dr. Martin Luther King, Jr. meant when he said in his "I Have a Dream" speech that he hoped that we would reach a point in this country when a man is judged by the content of his character and not by the color of his skin.

The story of Lamar Weaver's life and contribution to the Civil Rights Movement is told in mostly his own words and from his memory. I had the honor and privilege to make a small contribution in getting Rev. Weaver's story written and published. It is his desire that we jointly dedicate the book in the memory of his mother Mrs. Ruby Aileen Harris Weaver and in the memory of my dear mother and my best friend Mrs. Victoria.

Rueben Jackson

Introduction

"This is a good day to die you nigger loving son of a bitch." "You White bastard." These were only two of the many threats that rang out from the angry mob that had gathered at the Birmingham Terminal Railway Station in Birmingham, Alabama. It was Wednesday Morning, March 6, 1957. This is a day I will never forget, I heard these and many other threats before that day was over.

Lamar Weaver

Adversity is said to be the driving force of all great leaders and all great movements. On June 1, 1956 Alabama Attorney General John Patterson obtained a court order banning most of NAACP activity within the entire State of Alabama, including fund raising, dues collecting and other activities. [i] In response to this, Fred

---

i Parting the Waters, Taylor Branch 1988

Shuttlesworth, a local Black minister founded and became the first President of the Alabama Christian Movement for Human Rights, a pro-integration organization. The Alabama Christian Movement for Human Rights was established after the National Association for the Advancement of Colored People was outlawed in Alabama in 1956. The Alabama Christian Movement was also a forerunner of the Southern Christian Leadership Council. Reverend Shuttlesworth had also been the Pastor of the Bethel Baptist Church in North Birmingham since 1953. Shuttlesworth had been a pioneer in the Civil Rights movement having led many demonstrations. Once he and 20 other Blacks were arrested for attempting to integrate the buses in Birmingham in 1956. I had known Fred Shuttlesworth for several years and supported him in his efforts to end segregation. On the night of March 5, 1957 Fred Shuttlesworth called and told me what he planned to do the following day. He told me he intended to go and challenge the ordinance that forbade Blacks to sit-in the White waiting room at the Birmingham Terminal Railway Station. I welcomed his call. The time had come when the walls of segregation had to come down.

The next morning, I left my house on 11th Avenue North and drove down to the Terminal Railway Station. I parked a block north of the station and walked to the main entrance. There was a crowd of angry Whites milling around the Terminal Station. Among them was a pro-segregationist named R.E. Chambliss who was a leader of the Ku Klux Klan in the Birmingham area. R.E. Chambliss was linked to many of the terroristic acts in Birmingham including in many of the violent acts perpetrated against Black churches in the area (Chambliss was convicted years later for the murder of the four young Black girls at the 16th Street Baptist Church). R.E.Chambliss also known as Bill, knew me and when he saw me walk toward the entrance of the Terminal Station, he screamed out "this is a good day to die you nigger loving son-of-a-bitch." I walked into the station and over to where Rev. Fred Shuttlesworth and his wife Ruby were. They were sitting in the waiting room which was clearly marked "White Interstate Waiting Room." A short distance from where we were sitting, you could see the sign "Negro Waiting Room." White and Negro waiting rooms were customary all across America in those days, and especially in the South. I walked up to the Rev. and Mrs. Fred Shuttlesworth and shook their hands. I sat down and we started talking. Rev. Fred Shuttlesworth told me they had purchased tickets to Atlanta and were going for a visit. While I was talking with the Shuttlesworths, the mob that was gathering outside was growing in size and intensity. They were screaming insults at the three of us, Rev. and Mrs. Fred Shuttlesworth and me. As the mob got larger, some of them moved inside taking up a large portion of the White waiting room. The mob was led by none other than R.E. Chambliss.

As the tension mounted, I felt that an attack by the mob was imminent. In the ensuing chaos, a few policemen tried to maintain order. A policeman walked up and asked Rev. Shuttlesworth if they had tickets which Rev.

Shuttlesworth produced. The police asked me if I had a ticket and when I said no, the policeman grabbed my arm and said "let's go" and escorted me to the door. At the front entrance of the railway station, he ordered me to go outside. There was a mob of angry White men who met me at the door. They began cursing and threatening me. One person in the mob screamed "hand him over to us" while another voice cried out "this is judgment day for you, you bastard." A police officer pushed me out on to the sidewalk and the door closed behind me. I was surrounded by this angry mob. I was terrified. I turned toward the area where my car was parked and started walking slowly toward my car. The mob was so close to me, I could feel their hot breath on the back of my neck. I knew if I ran I would most certainly be killed much like a pack of wild dogs would do when they chase after their prey. Then suddenly, someone hit me from behind with a suitcase and knocked me to the ground. Some of the persons in the mob begin kicking me. I struggled back to my feet trying desperately to make it to my car. The mob followed me. The news media were there taking pictures. Thank God for those reporters, if they had not been there with their cameras, I'm sure I would have been killed. Getting to my car seemed like an eternity. Finally, I made it and managed to somehow get inside. I fumbled with the keys as I attempted to get them into the ignition trying to get the car started. Finally I was able to get it started but I could not go forward because I was up against a building. And by now, the mob, who had continued to follow me, had surrounded my car like a swarm of angry bees. There were ten to fifteen men on each side of the car trying to flip it over on its top. At one point they had the wheels completely lifted up off the ground, about to tip the car over. My car was a convertible and had they succeeded I would probably have been crushed. When their efforts to turn my car over failed, they began throwing cement blocks on to the top of my car. Several cement blocks made their way into my window barely missing me. One of the cement blocks lodged in the right window of my car. I had to find a way to get out of there in a hurry, otherwise I would have been killed right on the spot. This was the first time in my life that I was literally almost frightened to death. I began to back slowly out of the parking lot. R. E. "Bill" Chambliss was standing at the front of my car inciting the mob to turn the car over. As I backed out, some members of the mob were shouting "kill him, kill the White son-of-a-bitch", still attempting to turn the vehicle over. At this point the rocking of my car had become more violent and I knew that any moment now and they were going to flip the car over. I could see Chambliss at the front of my car sneering and cursing and trying to help the mob turn my car over. At the same time other members of the mob were throwing rocks and some of the rocks made their way through the top of the car and the windows narrowly missing my head. As I backed the vehicle up to head out to the street, a man in the mob managed to open my car door and began striking me. A reporter taking pictures for the national media grabbed the man and pushed him away and slammed my car door shut. I hit the accelerator and sped away into the intersection. I must have struck one or two persons in the crowd as they continued to try to stop my car. I drove across 26th street, ran a red light and sped down 6th Avenue toward the police station. I rushed into the police station for help and to report the incident.

When I got inside of the police station, a funny thing happened. *I* was arrested and charged with reckless driving, running a red light and striking a pedestrian! I thought I had reached safety, instead I was arrested for reckless driving and endangering a pedestrian. Such was the depth of injustice in those days. I asked for a speedy trial and was taken into the courtroom of City Judge Oliver B. Hall. During the trial the judge admonished me for my support of integration. He told me "a man can not fly into the face of traditions and customs and not expect to be burned." "You knew you shouldn't be there. You incited it. You helped stir it up. You certainly are guilty." I told the Judge I was fleeing for my life, this was apparently irrelevant. He fined me twenty-five dollars and told me to get out of town. I will never forget standing in front of Judge Hall who chastised me for being in the wrong place at the wrong time. I was dumfounded, still scared and could not believe what had just happened. Police commissioner Bull Connor sent me a message while I was still in the courtroom. "Leave Birmingham as soon as possible your life is in danger, they are going to try and kill you." I assumed he meant the Ku Klux Klan.

John and Ernest Poole were brothers who owned Poole Funeral Home, a Black owned business there in Birmingham. They came and paid my fine. One of the

Poole brothers had driven my car from city hall and hidden it. The other brother drove me to the Poole Funeral Home. I hid there for the rest of the day and that night. A Negro informant told the police that I was hiding at the Poole Funeral Home. When they couldn't find me there, the mob continued their search for me throughout the city. At least twice during the late hours of the night, angry Whites came into the funeral home looking for me. Aubry Thomas, Rev. Addie White and Aubry Bushelon three employees of the Poole Funeral Home had hidden me in a casket.

Thursday night, March 7, 1957, Aubry Thomas and Aubry Bushelon took me to the airport, where I was to fly to Washington to appear before a Senate Judiciary Sub-Committee on Civil Rights that was trying to put together the first Civil-Rights Bill. Rev. Shuttlesworth and I had been invited to go to Washington. I made reservations under the fictitious name of *James Bishop* in an effort to keep my trip to Washington a secret and to keep my whereabouts unknown. Despite these precautions someone found out I was going to the airport. When we arrived at the airport and I picked up my ticket, I was informed that someone had phoned in a bomb threat. After a delay to check for a possible bomb, we departed without further incident and arrived several hours later in Washington in the early morning hours of March 8 , 1957. I was still in fear from the previous day's events all the way to Washington, I just knew this was going to be my day to die. I thought about all of the threats on my life that had been made the previous day and felt like this was going to be my judgment day.

In The Beginning

During the flight I reflected back on the days and the events that had led up to the dangerous incident that had taken place at the Terminal Station. I started thinking about this mission that God had given me and I wondered where was it going to end. My thoughts led me back to my early childhood. I was born January 11, 1928 in a small southern town called Cassville. Cassville is located in Bartow County, Georgia. Cassville is located a little north of Atlanta. My mother's name was Ruby Aileen Harris Weaver. My father, who was a farmer, was named Almos Weaver. I was born on what was known in these parts as the "Price Place." The Price Place was just a short stone's throw from the Cassville Cemetery in Cassville. My father was from Arab, Alabama but when he married my mother he was living in a little town called Holly Pond, Alabama. I don't remember much about my early childhood, except, one event that is still vivid in my mind. My father and mother were returning with me in an old Ford from Cassville to Holly Pond, Alabama. This was one of many trips we made between Georgia and Alabama during my early childhood. On this particular occasion, I was about four years old and we were traveling down an old dirt road near Center, Alabama. I thought it must have been on a weekend because as we approached a crossroad I saw a large group of people standing around in a festive like atmosphere. There were so many people that they were partially blocking the road. As we drew closer, I was not prepared for what I was about to see. I witnessed one of the most horrific things I have ever seen even to this day. What I witnessed was a horrible experience for me. As our car stopped, we saw some White men, some dressed in robes, standing on a platform with a young Negro boy who I think could have been anywhere from fifteen to eighteen years old. There he was standing stripped of his clothing and the Whites were savagely beating him. Then they brought out axes and they began hacking his body to pieces, killing him before our very eyes. It was like a slaughterhouse. Blood was everywhere. My father, mother and I watched in horror. I remember my mother crying. I just sat there horrified. It was a sight I will remember for the rest of my life. Looking back now, that experience made an impact on my life that may have been the reason my life took the path that it did.

Shortly after witnessing that horrifying tragedy, we moved from Holly Pond to Cullman, Alabama. We lived there for a short time and then moved on to Birmingham. The first time we drove into the City of Birmingham, I remember seeing a big sign on the outskirts of the city that said "Birmingham, the Magic City of the South", and I remember another sign that said "Birmingham the Pittsburgh of the South." One of the places that we lived was located at 1712 7th Avenue

North. We moved around a lot and lived in several areas of Birmingham. When I started school, however, I remember we were living on 7th Avenue North, by then my mother and father had separated and gotten a divorce. My mother enrolled into nursing school at the old Hillman Hospital and she had enrolled me in Henley Elementary School at 17th Street and 6th Avenue. I have some fond memories during my time at Henley. My principal's name was Mrs. Green. The playground where we played across the street from Henley was called Kelly Ingram Park. Kelly Ingram Park was a significant landmark because it was also the boundary that separated the Black neighborhood from the White neighborhood. In those days I hung out with a White street gang in the area. There were both White and Black gangs of about equal number. Some of the members of my gang had guns and knives but mostly we fought with rocks. Most of fights took place in and around Kelly Ingram Park. Even though Kelly Ingram Park was bordered on one side by the Black neighborhood, the park was segregated. Two of my friends were brothers named Eddie and Bobbie Potts. We were members of the same gang. However, my very best friend was a young Black boy whose name was David Cross. He was a member of a Black gang and I met him because we both hung around an Italian owned grocery store at 8th and 17th David came from a poor family and some mornings on my way to school, I would meet David and share my lunch, which generally consisted of two biscuits. David did not go to school. There were no Blacks in Henley School. David and I would meet sometime in the afternoon at 8th and 17th and steal fruit from the grocery store. Once we got caught and the owner thrashed us both with a stick. Not long after that, David was hit by a streetcar and died shortly afterward. They took his body to either Poole Funeral Home or Mary E. Strong Funeral Home. I remember going to David's funeral. I picked some flowers on the way and took them to the funeral home. I remember everybody at the funeral home was trying to comfort me by telling me that David had gone to heaven. Later that same night, I went back to the store where David was killed and threw a brick through the grocery window. I remember hollering out loud "this is for David." We moved a lot during my youth. I finished Henley School and then went on to Phillips High School and finally Ensley High School. I was still traveling once or twice a year back to Cassville, Georgia where I also attended Cassville Schools during those brief periods I had to stay there. Whenever I was living in Cassville, I had to help my uncle on the farm.

Crossroads

When I returned to Birmingham, I worked at a variety of odd jobs over the years. I worked at Luquire Funeral Home in Norwood when I was about twelve years old. I started there at twelve dollars per week as an ambulance attendant. I was considered a big child for my age so I could do the work. When I got old enough to get my driver's license I became an ambulance driver. I worked for a number of different funeral homes including Johns Service Funeral Home on 7th Avenue North and for Wright Funeral Home. It was during this time that I first met and became friends with Ernest and John Poole.

After I had worked a while for those other companies, I decided to start my own ambulance service. With the help of James Poole I bought an old hearse. That business did not last long. Congressman Luther Patrick befriended me and got me a temporary job with the post office during the winter of 1946. My job with the post office came to an abrupt end because of a stupid prank that turned out to not be so funny. Another young man and I thought it would be a joke to take some of the 3rd and 4th class bags of mail and dump them into the Cahaba River. It turned out to be a big mistake. We were caught and I was charged with

embezzlement. My lawyer tried to convince the prose-
cutor that nothing was embezzled, and it was just a stupid practical joke, but I was convicted and sentenced to
serve eighteen months in El Reno Federal Reformatory,
El Reno, Oklahoma. The sentencing date was June 27,
1947. After I served fourteen months, I received a con-
ditional release on August 8, 1948. After I was released,
I went back home to Cassville, Georgia and worked on
the farm with my uncle.

When I think back on it, my unfortunate run in with
the law was probably a blessing in disguise. During
those fourteen months in reformatory, I had an opportunity to do a lot of soul searching. Since there was not
much happening back home in Cassville, I went with a
young companion one night to the People's Valley
school to a church revival where the most important
event in my whole life occurred. I remember the
preacher, a Reverend Lee Black, preaching an old-fash-
ioned gospel sermon that convinced me that my life was
headed in the wrong direction. He preached the kind of
sermon that makes you think that the preacher is
preaching only to you. When Rev. Black gave the altar
call, I got up from my seat and ran down the aisle to the
altar. All I could think of was that I wanted to accept
the Lord as my Savior. Tears of joy flowed down my
face as my mind flashed back with thoughts of a young
boy named David, my childhood friend, who had been
killed some years earlier. I wanted to be in a position to
go to heaven to see him. The memories of what took
place there when I accepted the Lord in my life is for-
ever etched in my mind. After that night, I joined the

Oak Grove Baptist Church that was located near Cass Station, Georgia where I was baptized a short time later. I remained in Cassville for another full year working on the farm and going to church. I missed my mother and I wanted to go back to Birmingham.

Birmingham 1949

In the autumn of 1949, I returned to Birmingham, by then my mother had graduated from the Hillman Nursing School. She was living in Norwood and working as a private duty nurse. I had been gone for over fifteen months and I wanted to get a job to help her and to get on with my life. I stayed away from the guys in the old gang. I didn't run the streets. I stayed out of trouble. I wasn't the "smart alec" that I had been in the past. I was a completely changed person. After my conversion, I started a new life, the old things that I did were no longer appealing to me. I wanted to do something worthwhile, starting with helping my mother. I started going to church at the Norwood Baptist Church. I even started going to Sunday School. I went every Sunday. I remember a couple that sang at the church, Mr. and Mrs. Hasty. Mr. Hasty sang like George Beverly Shea. He was a great singer and I enjoyed hearing him sing. I enjoyed the fellowship of going to church and meeting new people.

I renewed my friendship with Ernest and John Poole, who owned the Poole Funeral Home. I had no idea at this time what role the Pooles would play just a few years later to save my life. Around this time I took on a variety of jobs. I became a door-to-door Bible salesman.

I also sold Kirby vacuum cleaners door-to-door. I even sold pillows in those days door-to-door. Then I got a job with L&N Railroad. I worked the line that ran between Birmingham and New Orleans. I would go down during the week and come back on weekends. Things were really going well in those days. I was happy and I also made sure that I took the time to get involved with a group at my church. Some of the fellow members of that group were attending Southeastern Bible College. Southeastern Bible College was originally started in 1935. At that time it was simply known as the School of the Bible. The name was later changed to Southeastern Bible College. A man by the name of Dr. Charles Sidenspinner was President from 1945 to 1958. Southeastern Bible College is still active today. It is a great college in Birmingham and it has sent hundreds of missionaries all around the world. On one occasion, I went over with the group to meet Dr. Sidenspinner. Dr. Sidenspinner was a short man who wore glasses. His physical stature did not reflect his greatness. One of Dr. Sidenspinner's favorite subjects was the Book of Revelations.

Throughout this period, I was praying for God to reveal to me what He wanted me to do with my life. I wanted to enroll in class but I did not have the price of tuition. Despite this fact, Dr. Sidenspinner was kind enough to allow me to sit-in on his classes. As an unofficial student not formally enrolled, my name did not appear on the register until 1951 or 1952 and maybe parts of 1953. Eventually, I did formally enroll and I received some credits for my attendance. Southeastern

Bible College was a great experience for me because it put me in touch with a real Christian Group. The group was a highly motivated group of young men and women who seemed to love the Lord. The members of the group were studying not only for the ministry but to become missionaries. I had felt for sometime that God had wanted me to do something like this and that he wanted me to get actively involved. While I was a member of the Norwood Baptist Church, I felt the call to preach.

Early Transitions

While members of my church group were attending Southeastern Bible College, we began to hear almost daily what was happening within the Civil Rights Movement in the South. We witnessed how Blacks were mistreated in every walk of life. Even an attempt by a Black to drink at a "White only" water fountain could cost him or her their life. Two Black couples were arrested and beaten after they attempted to sit-in at the lunch counter at J.J. Newberry's in downtown Birmingham, Alabama. Incidents such as this were becoming more and more common place. The buses were also segregated throughout the south. This applied to all forms of public transportation, interstate and intrastate. Blacks and Whites could not mix in any social activities. The situation was so terrible that the mere *asking* for equal treatment and equal education would trigger terrorist acts against Blacks by the Ku Klux Klan. Many Negro homes and churches were burned to the ground. In fact, even moderate Whites who attempted to challenge the Jim Crow laws risked losing status and social positions within their community. In many cases the penalty was even higher if one persisted with any opposition to segregation.

The depths of hatred and fear of many of the segregationists could not be characterized as less than barbaric and maniacal. In fact, many of the things that were done to preserve the status quo of segregation would have been almost comical if they were not so tragic and violent. One such case involved a Black man by the name of Hartman Turnbow[1] who lived on a farm outside of Mileston, Mississippi. Hartman Turnbow became a target by the Klan after he became the first Black man to attempt to register to vote in one hundred years in Holmes County Mississippi. Hartman Turnbow's house was firebombed while he and his family lay asleep. When they tried to escape the flames the White perpetrators fired a barrage of bullets into the house to keep them from escaping the flames. Hartman Turbow returned fire and managed to drive the would-be assassins away. The Sheriff of Holmes County Mississippi, Andrew P. Smith, arrested not the White perpetrators who had firebombed and shot up the house, but Hartman Turnbow himself. He accused Hartman Turnbow of firebombing and shooting up his own house to gain sympathy. Even if one could buy into that ridiculously convoluted lunacy, who in the hell did Sheriff Smith think would be sympathetic? Certainly not the Whites. There were literally hundreds

1 Parting the Waters pg. 781

of such incidents of violence taking place across the south with similar outcomes.

The police and fire departments were completely segregated in the City of Birmingham. Lynchings were everywhere. In Mississippi, alone it was reported that there were over one thousand lynchings. In Alabama and Georgia there were several thousand more lynchings. I often joined with the other members of the group to pray and talk about it and we asked God to direct us. We finally came to the conclusion that God wanted us to go out and do something, take a stand, right some wrongs, talk Black people and encourage them to register to vote. Two other students at Southeastern Bible College joined me and we would make trips into the countryside on weekends. We spent a lot of time visiting smaller towns in Alabama. I remember one trip we made down to Evergreen, Alabama. In Evergreen we talked to the owner of the local Black-owned funeral home and he introduced us to several residents of the area. Our message in the beginning was simple. We made the point to Blacks that a person is not a first-class citizen until they become a registered voter. We told them that they could not bring about change in their life styles unless they were registered to vote.

Even before I had become actively involved in the Civil Rights Movement I had developed many friendships and relationships with people in the Black community especially among Black funeral directors. These relationships and experiences proved to be invaluable in our working in the Civil Rights Movement. There were times when we were able to preach in some of the local Black churches in those small towns. We would also go back to those small towns to check on their progress. Sometimes our efforts produced favorable results and a few would manage to register. But more often than not we heard horror stories about how they had attempted to register to vote in various counties throughout Alabama, Mississippi, Georgia and Florida and were punished for it. There were many accounts of how many of these people were beaten, threatened and had their houses or churches bombed and burned. At some of the voter registration places, the White registrars would create many bogus tests and fabricate other requirements Blacks would have meet in order to qualify to register to vote. For example, in Mississippi, registrars would tell Blacks attempting to register to recite the Mississippi Constitution, spell Mississippi backwards and to name all the presidents of the United States. There was even a test question requiring that Blacks to tell how many bubbles were in a bar of soap! Even if Blacks were able to meet qualifications, they would still be turned away saying that quotas had been reached for that day. Many White registrars would refuse to allow Blacks to register to vote under any circumstances. Some of them would refuse even if it meant leaving their jobs.

My two young friends and I had success in and around Phoenix City, Alabama and Columbus, Georgia. We also made some inroads in Meridian, Mississippi and Columbus, Mississippi. We talked to a small congregation in Union, Mississippi and while there we asked questions about the number of registered voters in Newton and Neshoba Counties. Apparently as word got out about our efforts, someone notified the local Sheriff. When we were leaving town we stopped for gas. As we pulled away from the gas station we were stopped by two cars marked "Sheriff." Some of the men were in uniform and some were not. They asked us what we were doing in that area. I knew if I didn't think of a good answer quick we would be in trouble. I said we were with the FBI and they let us go. One weekend we were near Fort Walton Beach, Florida where we had visited a Black couple who lived near Eglin Air Force Base. We were on the way from Fort Walton Beach, Florida to visit my mother and stepfather who were living in Crestview, Florida, when out of no where came this car. Even though they were behind us we could see that they had white sheets over their heads. They were honking their horns and we heard gun shots as we sped down the highway. We were in my Cadillac convertible, which was not a new car, but it was a good car and I was trying to out run them, but they still managed to catch up with us from behind and hit my bumper. They tried to go around us on a two-lane road as this happened. Fearing for our lives, I would move over to keep them from going around. At least seven shots were fired. One bullet hole was later found in the top of my car. I never will forget when one of the young men said to me "Brother Weaver, let's pull over and pray with these people." I said Brother, I will let you out and let you pray with them but I am not going to stop." As we reached the city limits of Crestview, I started blowing my horn to get attention. It was at that point the Klan turned around and went back in the opposite direction. They didn't want to be seen. My car had been hit by several bullets. We were trembling with fright. We stopped to pray as soon as we reached a safe haven. We thanked God He had spared our lives because we had come very close to death that day.

Another equally harrowing experience occurred in Laurel, Mississippi. We were en-route back to Alabama when we heard a police siren behind us. We pulled over and four men approached us with their guns drawn. The wanted to know what we were doing there. I said, "we are members of the White Citizens Council." Someone said praise God and they let us go. Those were extremely dangerous times when the lives of Blacks and anyone who attempted to bring about change was in danger. Somehow, God gave me the courage to carry on.

Gathering Momentum

Back in Birmingham, I had gotten a job at Tennessee
Coal and Iron Company (TCI), in Fairfield and I
resumed my studies at Southeastern Bible College,
when possible. One day the President called me into
his office to deliver a message. The President said that
he had received a call from Thomas J. Gardner who
was the manager of the Smith & Gaston funeral home
down on 16th Street. He said that Mr. Gardner had
expressed a desire to have someone come and speak to
his employees in the chapel of the funeral home and
my name had been mentioned. I accepted the invitation and a few days later I had the privilege to go to
speak to the Smith & Gaston employees. In attendance
were several members of Mr. Gastons Insurance
Company and most of the funeral home employees.
They assembled in the chapel of their building. I think
the funeral home was across from the Kelly Ingram
Park. The topic of my sermon was the Christian decision. I spoke about my own personal experiences and
told them that in life we come to many cross roads
when we must sometimes make difficult decisions. I
spoke about how important it is to make the right decision and not just the right decision but the Christian
decision. I told them to pray and talk to God about the
direction they should take. After I finished, the group

gathered around and very enthusiastically congratulated me. I just felt great that I had been able to come
down, meet with these people and speak.

This was my first time meeting with Thomas J.
Gardner, who I later learned to call "T J." Thomas
Gardner helped me in my voter registration activities by
giving me the names of people to contact in small towns
in Alabama and some in Georgia. My two young asso-
ciates and I used those contacts at one time or another.
Thomas Gardner became a life-long friend. Thomas
Gardner was A.G. Gaston's brother-in-law. A.G.
Gaston was the owner and president of A.G. Gaston
Funeral Homes and one of the most powerful Blacks in
Alabama. A.G. Gaston also became a friend. I visited
him several times in his home and with his family. He
became a tremendous supporter of mine. He was a
friendly man who spoke with conviction. I will never
forget the words he shared with me, "do what God tells
you to do and you will make good". Neither will I forget T. J. Gardner for his help in those early days in
Birmingham. I also remember Emory Jackson who was
the editor of the Birmingham World. Emory and I
would have a meeting every time I would come back
into Birmingham from one of our voter registration
trips out of town. We would meet with Emory in a
small office that he had up on 17th Street. He would
pull the blinds because of fear that if White people saw
us together they would throw a brick through his window. He was always afraid of being shot because he
had been threatened. He was a great friend and advisor
throughout the years in Birmingham and I never have

forgotten Emory. Although Emory and T.J. both have gone on to be with the Lord, the memories of them are still fresh on my mind.

Head to Head with Bull Connor

I married a young lady from Huntsville, Alabama who was a student nurse at the Methodist Hospital in Norwood. Out of that marriage came a daughter, Linda Christine. I continued working at the TCI. I was still attending Southeastern Bible College, when possible. My two young friends and I were still making weekend excursions attempting to get people to register to vote. Some of us at the school were horrified to read daily newspaper accounts of how Blacks were being beaten and jailed around Birmingham. I stood up at school and spoke to a small group and said it is time for some-one to speak up and condemn this sort of action. Someone said, "why don't you run for public office". I began to think about this and talked to both my White and Black friends seeking their input before I began my campaign. I went to visit Rev. Fred Shuttlesworth, who was the pastor of Bethel Baptist Church. I remember the day I went to his church in North Birmingham. I walked in and this young man came out. I said, "I am here to see your father, the Rev. Fred Shuttlesworth can you help me?" The young man told me "I am Rev. Fred Shuttlesworth." I was amazed that he was so young. We talked and he showed me a plaque on the wall at the entrance of the church that listed names of people who had registered to vote. "I am trying to register all of my people to vote and I emphasize that they are not first-class citizens until they are registered to vote."

The time for the Democratic Primary was approaching. This would be a chance for someone to challenge Bull Connor. I prayed about it and I spoke to one of my best friends in the Black community named Virgil Harris. Virgil advised me to run for office. Virgil owned the Davenport and Harris funeral home. Virgil was also president of Protective Life Insurance Company. When I did decide to run, Virgil was my campaign manager. He raised quite a bit of money. We used the funds to buy newspaper ads, radio time and window cards. It was ironic that Virgil was better qualified than I in every respect, yet, as unqualified as I was, I entered the race. As I think back, I must have been crazy to challenge Bull Connor but I was on a mission from God. It was a challenge for me to run for City Commissioner in Birmingham, but I had never backed down from a challenge. Bull was first elected in 1937, but declined to run again in 1953. The reason Bull Connor had decided to not run that year was because of a sex scandal in which he was involved. Henry Darnell, a rival police officer,[2] had discovered the affair and crashed the door down at

2 Parting the Waters, footnote pg. 644

the Tutweiler Hotel where he exposed Bull Connor in a room with his secretary. That scandal almost ruined Bull Connor. Connor was arrested and convicted on morals charges and run out of office. In 1955, after a one-term absence, Bull was ready to go again. Bull Connor was an absolute segregationist. To him Blacks were inferior and had no rights whatsoever. He enforced this with his all White police force. I determined it was time for a change. The campaign began in earnest.

I put political signs up all over the City of Birmingham. I called for the hiring of Blacks on the police force and the fire department. I campaigned hard. I spoke about the issues and, because of good advice that Virgil Harris gave me, I told the voters the truth. Virgil arranged for me to meet with the leaders of the Black community. I was told that Black leaders supported me but could not openly endorse me for fear of reprisal from Bull Connor and others. I said I would raise salaries in the police and fire department and I would recoup that money with recycling. On several occasions, as I traveled around campaigning, Whites threw rocks at my car on several occasions, when I would leave my car, I would return to find that my tires were flat. On more than one occasion I was even shot at on the porch of my home on 29th Street North. The situation became so dangerous that my father in law came down from Huntsville, Alabama and took my wife and daughter to Huntsville because he feared for their lives. Later my wife divorced me and changed my daughter's name. This was a real difficult time for me and everyday that I continued to run the campaign, I knew that it very well could have been my last.

On Christmas night 1956, Fred Shuttlesworth's church and home were bombed. I heard it on the radio and rushed from my residence on 11th Avenue North over to his church. The marauders had destroyed most of his house and severely damaged the church. I thought this was a terrible thing to have happen at Christmas time. When Christians should show their love for Christ, but this bunch was out bombing the churches and homes of Black ministers. I later told that story to the Senate Sub-Committee in Washington, DC.

My campaign for the Birmingham City Commission was going well. My radio spots were well written, thanks to Virgil. We were running numerous newspaper ads, thanks to Virgil Harris's ability to get union support, raise money to pay for them. I thought that because I worked for TCI I would get some union support so I spoke to several White union groups. They had one major concern, they wanted to understand my reason for hiring Blacks on the police force, which I gave and they seemed to understand. Virgil and I thought that we would do no worse than third in this five man race. My four opponents had labeled me a nigger lover and a communist.

On election night we did not have to wait long for a clear result. Bull Connor was first, Jabo Waggner was second, and I trailed third. I told Virgil that I got 3,149

Black votes. He said, "but you got 3,150 votes" I said,
"yes I know I voted for myself." Bull Connor and Jabo
Waggner both had over spent their allotted expense for
the campaign. The problem for them was they had not
listed all of their campaign contributions and expendi-
tures. I reported this to the press and protested to the
election commission. However, the election commission
decided to up hold the election results. Nevertheless, I
was granted the right to run again in the run-off as a
write-in candidate. This brought a lot of reaction from
both Bull Connor and Jabo Waggner. They got their
pencils sharpened and came back with all kinds of new
figures. It also created a tremendous amount of reaction
from the press. It also created anger towards me among
some of the hate groups in the area especially the Klan,
and the North Alabama Citizens Council. The events
that followed made it unsafe for me to continue my
campaign. I left Birmingham before that election. I did
not win but Bull Connor also lost the close election to
Jabo Waggner. Bull Connor did not run again until
1957 when he would be elected by a narrow margin.
Sad however was the fact that not only had I lost the
election but my family as well. [The shots fired into my
house could have been fatal. The bullets had also come
close to my family. When we called the police they
showed up about four hours later. Nothing was ever
done about it. I was glad my father-in-law had come
and moved my family to Huntsville because it was too
dangerous for them to live in Birmingham with me.]

Meeting Harry S. Truman

Former President Harry S.Truman was returning to Missouri from a vacation in Florida and was passing through Birmingham. While in Birmingham, he decided that he would like to meet with Rev. Fred Shuttlesworth and me. We were notified by someone, who I don't remember, that the former President's private car would be at the Terminal Station on a side track for an hour or so and we could go down and see him. I called Fred to let him know and then we both went down to the Terminal Station to meet with former President Harry Truman. We had our picture taken with him by the side of his private car. The picture ran in the *Birmingham News*. Former President Truman remarked to Fred that he was very excited about all of his Civil Rights activities. He congratulated me for my stand and he told us to keep up our fight for human rights. He encouragingly told us that these ugly hate groups would pass. He said that even though he had left the White House he would do all he could to further our efforts and help in trying to correct a lot of wrongs. We spent about fifteen or twenty minutes talking to the former President at the Union Terminal in Birmingham. I was amazed that he knew so much about what was going on and I was equally amazed that he was very interested in our cause. He expressed regrets to Fred because he knew that his home and church had been bombed. He told us that he would ask the FBI to look into the incident. He further added that these were violent times and to be very, very careful. His last words to us were "God Bless you." I felt humbled and remember saying to Fred "do you realize that Harry Truman stopped in Birmingham and we were the only two people he talked to?" Fred remarked that he felt good about that meeting and so grateful that someone like President Truman would take an interest in human rights. Little did I know that a few days later the KKK would strike at the Terminal Station and that Fred and I would both be the targets.

Henley School
Birmingham,
Alabama

Young Lamar
Weaver 1940

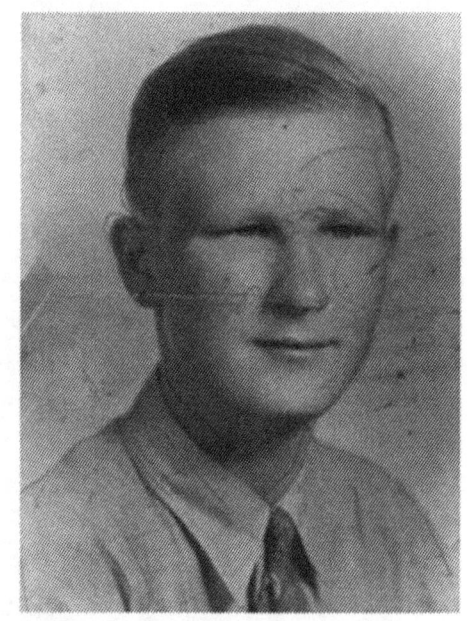

Rev. Lamar
Weaver 1955

President Harry S.
Truman, Rev.
Shuttlesworth and
Rev. Lamar
Weaver, 1957
Birmingham,
Alabama

Mrs. Materia Poole
and Rev. Weaver at
the Poole Funeral
Chapel

Rev. Weaver at
Poole Funeral
Chapel with coffin
much like the one
used to hide him
from the mob in
1957

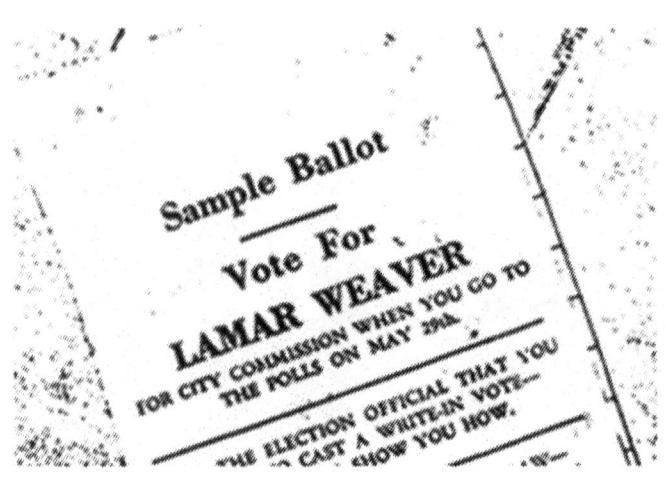

Rev. Shuttlesworth and
Rev. Weaver at the
Birmingham Civil Rights
Museum

Plaque displayed in
Birmingham Civil
Rights Museum

March 6, 1957

Lamar Weaver, a White
integrationist, tests
segregation of Birmingham's
train terminals.

Birmingham City Councilman, Aldrich Gunn and Rev. Lamar Weaver

Rev. Weaver, Rev Shuttlesworth an Mrs. Materia Poole

City of Birmingham
Mayor Arrington,
Mrs. Materia Poole,
Rev. Weaver and
First Lady Arrington

Georgia State
Representative John
White, City of Atlanta
Mayor Bill Campbell
and Rev. Weaver

Rev. Fred
Shuttlesworth

Rev. Lamar Weaver at
Town Hall meeting
Birmingham, Alabama
May 2000

Rev. Lamar
Weaver and Dr.
Horace Huntley

Rueben Jackson,
Rev. Fred
Shuttlesworth
and Rev. Lamar
Weaver

Birmingham Mayor
Richard Arrington & City
Council President Bell

Reverend Lamar Weaver
and Birmingham,
Alabama City Council
President Bell

Washington

When the plane landed in Washington on March 8, 1957 I went to the YMCA. Later in the morning I went to the capitol building and there found the Sub-Committee taking testimony on the first Civil Rights Bill. As I sat in the waiting room to make my statement, the congressman from Birmingham, George Huddleston, came up to me and said "Lamar don't ever go back to Birmingham, you'll never be welcomed. You are a disgrace. You are the most hated White man in the south." Additionally, he called me some other names I will not repeat. I made my statement, which is now a matter of record in the Congressional Archives. This is the statement to the Senate Judiciary Sub-Committee for proposed Civil Rights:

"Gentlemen:

My name is Lamar Weaver; I live at 1131 North 29th Street Birmingham, Alabama. I offer this statement to the Senate Judiciary Sub Committee for proposed Civil Rights legislation. When you cross the Mason Dixon line into the South you enter a foreign country, a country where violence and mob rule are king and the Ku Klux Klan hold open meetings in violation of the law against wearing hoods and robes. They also carry firearms without permits. One

incident I can give is a meeting in the month of
January 1957 in the Central Park Theater,
which is now rented and occupied by the North
Alabama Citizens Council. One Asa Carter
according to warrants sworn out by city detec-
tives did shoot with intent to murder not less
than one or more than two participants in a Ku
Klux Klan meeting that night. They were
Federated Ku Klux Klan of the confederacy.
They had rented the theater for that night and
they were holding a meeting with hoods and
according to the testimony given by the injured
parties or party that they were also carrying con-
cealed weapons. As to this date Asa Carter is
under 20,000.00 bond for the above named
charge. Witnesses testified in the case that Asa
Carter was hooded and robed. Another incident
took place on March 6th, 1957 at approximately 12:30 PM at the Terminal Station in
Birmingham, Alabama, I was mobbed and
kicked and struck with a suitcase. I had my car
rocked by an angry mob which numbered fifty
to a hundred or more, and on the same date and
the same time the Rev. F.L. Shuttlesworth and
his wife bought a ticket to Atlanta, Georgia and
sat in the White waiting room in the above
named station a mob of approximately three
hundred, some of them who identified themselves to me as Klansmen and one of them identified by the *Birmingham Post Herald and The
Birmingham News* as a known member of the
Ku Klux Klan, namely R. E. Chambliss. He was

seen shoving the Rev. Shuttlesworth twice, Chambliss was taken by the arm by a plain clothes detective, moved a few feet then released. The mob jeered and cursed the Rev. Shuttlesworth, his wife and me. The Rev. Shuttlesworth was also shoved by R.E. Chambliss as he entered the Terminal Station to purchase a ticket. Rev. Shuttlesworth then sat down in the White waiting room. I shook hands with him.

Shortly afterwards, I was attacked by a mob as I left the station. I enter at this time as evidence a copy of the *Birmingham Post Herald* of Thursday March 7, 1957 describing the above named events which occurred on March 6, 1957. The Rev. F. L. Shuttlesworth's home and church were bombed Christmas night 1956. Rev. Shuttlesworth is the leader of the Alabama Christian Movement for human rights and as such leader has led the Negroes in the legal attempts to outlaw segregation of the races in public transportation in Birmingham. I was a candidate for Public Improvements Commission in the City of Birmingham for the 1957 campaign. I ran on a pro-integration platform. After announcing my pro-integration status, I received threats not only to my life but also to the lives of individual members of my family. My family left the City of Birmingham and I had to leave the State of Alabama. I also ran for City Council in 1956, that's the City Commission, in the election of 1956 on the same platform and received

3,150 votes and placed third in a field of five candidates. I wish to make a brief statement in respect to jury duty in Dallas County Alabama. Only one Negro has ever served on a jury. In Monroe, Wilcox and Lowndes County Alabama, no Negroes have ever served on a jury. The Negro population in these counties outnumbered the White population. The counties of Lowndes and Wilcox Alabama do not have any Negro registered voters. Bullock County, Alabama has only five Negro voters. The Negro population in the twelve counties of the Black belt constitutes sixty-six per cent of the population in those counties of voting age. However, only two point twelve percent of the Negroes of voting age are registered. Every obstacle devised by man is used to prevent Negroes from registering. In Macon County, Alabama, a registered board member resigned before he would register a Negro to vote. The world famous Tuskegee Institute is located in this county. Thank you."

As I left the hearing room my congressman again confronted me. I never saw anybody as mad as that man was. He was livid with anger. While I was in Washington, I was invited to appear on several shows. I accepted an invitation from H.V. Kalkenborn, radio talk show host. Chet Huntley, a leading TV newscaster on NBC Television came by the station and handed me a special delivery letter that he had received from a man in Detroit, Michigan. Mr. Kalkenborn asked me why, as a White man, I had gotten involved in the Civil Rights

Movement. I told him I wanted to see a lot of wrongs made right and I knew that what I was doing was the right thing to do. On his show we discussed the murder of Emmett Till that occurred in Money, Mississippi in 1955. I told him my opinion was Emmett was killed by two red-necked scum bums. He said to me, "you are a very brave man" and I said to him no, I am a saved man, there is a difference. While there, I talked to representatives of *Ebony Magazine, Jet, The Amsterdam News* and *The New York Post*. I was offered a job by the *Amsterdam News* and given a press card. My job was to go back to the South and supply them with voter registration statistics in several southern states. *Ebony Magazine* in August of 1957 featured the story about me on their front cover as "the White Man Who Can't Go Home." I gratefully acknowledged the Blacks who had made it possible for me to make the trip to Washington, D.C. They were A.G. Gaston, Virgil Harris, John and Ernest Poole along with other Black businessmen in Birmingham who had contributed to a fund for my Washington trip. I will always appreciate this, for if it had not been for them funding my trip I would not have been there. Late Friday afternoon, I received an invitation from Eleanor Roosevelt to come to Hyde Park, New York and Visit the Roosevelt Estate. I decided I would make the trip there the following weekend.

Visit to Roosevelt Estate

I left Washington on Sunday. I had hired a car and a driver and we agreed on a fee of $50.00 a day and we started out toward Philadelphia. I remember when we left Philadelphia we got lost somewhere in upstate Pennsylvania. After getting new directions we were able to find our way there. We arrived in Hyde Park, New York early on Tuesday morning. We had two blowouts but, in general, we were in good shape. I did not know where the Roosevelt Estate was. All that I knew was that it was in Hyde Park.

I decided to call the Sheriff's Department. After a while, a car from the Duchess County Sheriff's Department showed up. They made some telephone calls, then and asked me who I was and where I was going. Shortly after that, a car came to meet us and lead us to the Roosevelt Estate. I remember there was a heavy fog coming from the Hudson River. We passed the FDR home, went about a mile, and drove up to a modest home where we were met in the driveway by a man who introduced himself the care taker. We parked our cars, the Sheriff had a few words with him, and he led me up to the house.

Mrs. Roosevelt met us at the door. I had only seen her in pictures and not in person, so I really did not recognize her as Eleanor Roosevelt. She was very pleasant. She welcomed me telling that she was very happy to meet me. Imagine that? She also told me she had written some things about me in her newspaper column as a result of the telephone conversation that we had when I called her from Washington the week past, (she would see that I got copies of the articles.) She was very much aware of what was going on in the South. She asked me if I was hungry and shortly after that we sat down in a very modest dining area. A middle-aged lady served us breakfast. Mrs. Roosevelt told me that we were very near the Catskill Mountains and West Point Military Academy. All I could see outside was a dense fog which came from the Hudson River. She told me that she was very busy. I can attest to that because the telephone was rang almost constantly. Additionally, a lady came in several times to give her notes and messages that were coming in while we were there.

Mrs. Roosevelt said that she wanted to get a first-hand account of what I knew of Rev. Vernon Johns of Montgomery, Alabama. I told her what I knew—I had met Vernon Johns twice. I told Mrs. Roosevelt that I thought that Vernon Johns was a very dedicated person and that his liberal stand, even in his own church, had made him unpopular. I told her that his idea in the very beginning was to boycott the buses, and for Black people to start their own businesses. He said that Black people should refuse to ride the buses. She was very impressed with what she knew of Vernon Johns. She had found herself and others inspired by the work of Rev. Vernon Johns. Her whole body seemed to quicken as she talked about Rosa Parks and the bus boycott situation in Montgomery. Mrs. Roosevelt said when she learned of the Rosa Parks' arrest she could empathize with Rosa Parks and with Black people and she understood why Blacks were demanding fair treatment. She said she could imagine herself as a Black person and she regretted that she could not have been there to participant in that historic action by Rosa Parks. Mrs. Roosevelt marveled at the fact that the act one person could sometimes motivate and inspire thousands of people. She said it was really something because after the message came across the news service that thousands of Blacks had refused to ride the buses in Montgomery, Alabama. She also wanted to know what I knew about the Emmett Till case, the 13-year-old student who was murdered and mutilated August 29, 1955. Mrs. Roosevelt said that this news was flashed across the world. She said that world opinion and sympathy was generated towards the Civil Rights Movement. We talked about Rev. Fred Shuttlesworth, Pastor of the Bethel Baptist Church in North Birmingham and his efforts and his stand. She wanted to know if I knew him and I told her that I did. I told her of some of the heroics of Rev. Shuttlesworth and about the attack by the angry mob that took place at the Birmingham Union Terminal, the place where Rev. Shuttlesworth and I had protested the segregated waiting rooms. Her face seemed to light up as I told her about our experience. She said because of people like Fred and me and Rosa Parks, who was everyone's champion, also Vernon Johns, who made those early efforts in Montgomery. She said these people would go down in history as being there in the beginning and that these people and their contributions would never be forgotten in the history of the Civil Rights Movement. She asked me if I knew Dr. Martin Luther King and I told her I had met him once and I thought he was a born leader. I sat there sipping a cup of coffee transfixed and awestruck. I wanted to pinch myself to see if I was dreaming and to see if I was actually there in the presence of this great woman. It was almost a religious experience. I wanted to kneel and touch the hem of her garment. I was so overcome by emotion. I think she sensed this because she put her hand on mine and said, "How would you like to take a tour of the Roosevelt Estate?" I was on the verge of tears. It was indeed the most memorable event that ever happened in my whole life.

We first drove down by the Hudson River, alongside, and in front of the Vanderbilt Estate. She asked me if I would like to go through the Vanderbilt Estate, but knowing she was a very busy person and going out of her way to make me happy, I said no. I would much rather see the Roosevelt home. She took me on a tour of Val-Kill, her modest home. Then she had the driver drive on the Roosevelt Estate grounds. This is where FDR lived during his lifetime. We got out of the car and walked into the house. She took me through the house and I will admit that my legs were wobbly at times and my eyes teary because of the things that she said about her life with the President. We walked out onto the grounds, into the rose garden and to the grave of Franklin D. Roosevelt. (He died April 12, 1945.) As I stood, I breathed a prayer. As we walked away she took my arm and if she told me once, she told me 10 times to be careful to watch for ticks as I could get Lyme disease.

We drove back to Val-Kill and we got out of the car. She led me over the stone house, which was the first building, and she told me about the factory that once prospered there. We then walked back over to her cottage and she asked me if I was hungry. I told her no because I knew how busy she was and I did not want to impose anymore on her kindness. I was also very tired and I was ready to get back to Washington. We stood there for a few minutes and I remember one of the last things she said to me. She said "I want to know why you, a White man, would get involved in all this?" I told her, "Mrs. Roosevelt, you are White and you have been involved all of your life, seeing that a lot of the wrongs that existed in the South were made right. I too, felt a calling." I told her about my conversion and that God had called me and given me a mission and that I, too, wanted to see a lot of wrongs made right. That it was wrong what has happening in the South. It was immoral. It was sinful and that it was high time that the government stepped in with more powerful implements, such as a Civil Rights Bill. That was the reason I came to Washington and testified before the Senate Committee and that I prayed to God that a good workable Civil Rights Bill would be passed by the Congress. She said she was going to use her influence and do everything she could to help. She wanted to know three of the reasons why I was involved in the Civil Rights Movement and I told her: (1) God had saved me and that I had known since my conversion that my involvement was the right thing to do; (2) Because I had been there and seen first hand so many of the injustices practiced in the South against the Negro and so many lynchings. I told her of the one murder I had witnessed as a child. And (3) I told her, "Mrs. Roosevelt, you have been part of change. I, too, want to be a part of change." I told her that I believed that because of efforts of people like her, Vernon Johns, Fred Shuttlesworth, Rosa Parks and others, that things were going to change. I asked her to remember me in her prayers. She said for me to do the same for her and she reached out, touched me again on the shoulder, leaned over, and gave me a peck on the cheek. We said good-bye and as I got in my car, then the tears came. Oh, how the tears came. I was so happy that God had given me this opportunity.

We got back to Washington some time on Thursday and I immediately went to the train station and boarded the train for Birmingham. I had to go back at least one more time. Upon arriving in Birmingham a day or so later, I went immediately to the Poole Funeral Home and decided to rest for a while. My friends had hidden my car and I could use it if I wanted to, but I did not want to be seen because the car could be recognized anywhere on the streets. So I stayed at the Poole Funeral Home until Monday and one of the Poole employees, I believer either Aubry Thomas or Aubry Bushelon, drove me over to one of the churches on the north side where the Alabama Christian movement for human Rights was meeting. We parked outside and he went in to tell Rev. Fred Shuttlesworth I was there. He came back out and told me that Fred said that the Birmingham Police were watching the meeting and it would best for me not to come in because he thought there might be trouble. Again, I was warned to get out of Alabama because my life was in danger.

That night I went back to the Poole Funeral Home, got in my car, and headed south. I drove overnight to Crestview, Florida where my mother and stepfather lived. I decided it might be a good idea for me to stay at a safe place where I thought it was safe in Crestview with my mother and step-father and catch up on some rest and maybe do a little writing for *Ebony Magazine* and for the *New Amsterdam News*. I started making some trips again into some of the small towns in Florida, Alabama and Mississippi just overnight trips contacting a few Black families talking about voter registration and then coming back to my mother's home. This had become my base. This went on for probably two and a half months. Then a dramatic thing happened on June 19, 1957. That night my mother woke us all up screaming that the house was on fire. We ran out only to find that the house was not on fire. It was my car. The Klan had placed a cross on the side of my car. It had burned and gone through the top of the car onto the seat and gutted the inside of my car. We ran out with water and put the fire out, but the car had been severely damaged inside. In order to drive it, I had to put Coca-Cola crates on the floor to sit on. I called the police and fire departments. They never showed up and never made a report. I thought my mother's house was a safe place, but it was not. *The Afro-American Newspaper* ran a story and a picture of my car.

The next day, I threw two suitcases in my car and drove to Pensacola, Florida. I sold my car for $50.00 to a Black funeral director and boarded a train which would take me to Birmingham, then to Huntsville, Alabama and then on to Ohio. Rev.George Sangster, Pastor of Revelation Baptist Church and his assistant, Rev. Aaron Bland met me at the railway station in Cincinnati, Ohio. Revelation Baptist Church was Cincinnati's largest Black church. I joined that church several weeks later.

The first Civil Rights Bill passed in Washington. It was not the best, but it was a beginning. I went to work in a funeral home in Cincinnati and later joined the John Hancock Mutual Life Insurance Company. I married again and fathered four children. In 1961 my pastor, Rev. George W. Sangster dropped dead one Sunday morning in the pulpit. I petitioned the pulpit committee to hear a young minister from Birmingham, the Rev. Fred Shuttlesworth. After hearing him, they issued a call for him to become their pastor. Fred accepted and joined Revelation in August of 1961. Fred became a leader in Cincinnati and continued his civil rights work throughout America.

Reflections

I looked across the Ohio River today. It has often been called the Mason-Dixon Line. I thought of how the slaves came across that river to be free. I looked across to the South to where my roots were. I had been a small part in the Civil Rights movement in the South. I thought about the times I had been shot at, mobbed, and how my family was taken away from me. However, I can think of a 100 names of those who played a more important part than I. I pray to God that I, in some small way, helped to bring about change for the betterment of mankind. I didn't return to the South for 20 years. It would be longer before I returned to Birmingham, The Magic City of the South—the South that I love.

Warriors of the Civil Rights Movement

In the 1950's I was often told that I should write a book and tell about the early days of the human rights struggle. One of those who told me to write a book was EMORY JACKSON, the editor of the Birmingham World newspaper. I remember telling him, "Emory, if I ever write a book, I am going to mention your name and tell about your contributions to the struggle." I also vowed that I would tell about the contributions of many people both men and women, who played a greater part than I did in the Movement, who did not receive recognition for their courage and contributions. I wanted to tell about them and I hope in this last chapter that I am able to highlight and remember them as they were.

I first met Emory Jackson in the early 1950's. I read many of his articles in the *Birmingham World* and admired him tremendously. I liked him most of all, because he was his own man. He was dedicated to Human Rights. We often sat together in his small newspaper office near the Mecca Hotel. Whenever I would come by for a visit, we would always have to close the window shades because there was always the threat of window smashings and drive-by attacks. It was he who encouraged me to run for public office against Bull Connor. And when I went to work in 1952 at the T.C.I., later U.S. Steel Company, he helped me get an old car. He advised me on all-important matters concerning the Civil Rights Movement. After I was mobbed at the railroad station on March 6, 1957 Emory was there and helped me when I went into hiding. Emory went with me to the T.C.I. a few days later to pick up my last check. Fred Shuttlesworth and I had been subpoenaed by Senator Tom Henning of Missouri to testify before a U.S. Senate subcommittee. He subpoenaed us by placing the notice in the *Birmingham News*. I testified before a U.S. Senate Subcommittee that was debating the first Civil Rights Bill. Emory helped me to prepare my testimony. Emory was a father figure to me and I will never forget him. My own father had warned me the mid 1950's to get out of the Civil Rights Movement and quit embarrassing the family. When my father died 15 years later my name was omitted from his obituary and I was told not to come to the funeral. I was completely left out of his will. I never contested his actions. EMORY JACKSON was as great a leader as those who marched and died in the South. I am proud to have called him my friend.

I must also acknowledge a man who has encouraged me and helped to write my autobiography JOE DICKSON, the present editor of the *Birmingham World*. Joe often has opened his office to me and made me welcome. I owe him a debt of gratitude.

JONATHAN DANIELS, was a civil rights worker and a young man I knew. In 1965, He was 26 years old and was killed in Lowndes County, Alabama as he assisted Blacks to register to vote. RICHARD MORRISROE, a Roman Catholic priest was also shot in the same incident, but he survived. They should be remembered.

REV. FRED L. SHUTTLESWORTH, JR. Words can not express my feelings for this great man. He was the leader of the early Civil Rights Movement. I pray that a movie will be made that will properly show the facts as to his life and his accomplishments in the early days of the Civil Rights Movement. I first met Rev. Shuttlesworth and his wonderful wife, Ruby, in about 1953 when he was the pastor of BETHEL BAPTIST CHURCH, in North Birmingham. I visited his church. I never will forget the day I met him. I knocked at the church door and a young man answered. I looked a him thinking that the must be the son of the pastor—a mere boy, I thought. I said, "I would like to see Rev. Shuttlesworth." He replied with a big smile, "I am Rev. Shuttlesworth." I was at Bethel because Rev. Shuttlesworth had emerged as the leader of the early movement for human rights. I found out that day that he also was a born-again Christian and as a human rights activist. He was also concerned about doing God's work. He had already made his mark on the local scene. He had appeared before Birmingham City Commission and demanded that they hire Negro policemen. In 1956 when the NAACP was outlawed in Alabama, Rev. Shuttlesworth founded the Alabama Christian Movement for Human Rights. It was my pleasure to become a member and I spoke at several of their meetings. I was perhaps the only White member at that time. When Dr. Martin Luther King, Jr. started the SCLC, Rev. Shuttlesworth became involved. Rev. Shuttlesworth had already made progress in attempts to desegregate the buses and to integrate the lunch counters in Alabama. Long before King came on the scene, he was being jailed in Birmingham for his Civil Rights activities. On December 25th, someone placed dynamite under his home and church and damaged both structures. I visited him and Mrs. Shuttlesworth that night. Rev. Shuttlesworth said, "If it takes being killed to get integration, I'll do just that thing, because God is with me." He also said and I will never forget it, "that dynamite had my name on it." It he does write a book, I hope the title of it is "That Dynamite Had My Name On It." There were two attempts to kill Rev. Shuttlesworth by dynamite. Rev. Shuttlesworth and I were mobbed at the Union Railroad Station in Birmingham. Fred Shuttlesworth also made early attempts to integrate the Birmingham Schools. I remember when he was badly beaten as he attempted to enroll his children at Phillips High School.

When the pastor of the Revelation Baptist Church in Cincinnati, Ohio died in the pulpit, I called Fred on the telephone and told him they were going to invite him to come and speak to the pulpit committee. They later called him to become their pastor. He accepted. I was glad because I believe he would have been killed had he remained in Birmingham. I had become a member of Revelation Baptist Church in 1957. I never knew a man in the Civil Rights Movement who took more abuse and survived than Fred Shuttlesworth. He is still active in the struggle today in Cincinnati, Ohio and travels worldwide. He is one of the few remaining persons that is still alive from the beginning of the early days of the struggles for Human Rights. Fred Shuttlesworth, walked side by side with Vernon Johns, Ralph David Abernathy, and other great men of the movement. When Dr. Martin Luther King, Jr. came on the scene Fred joined with him and became a faithful ally. When President Harry Truman came to Birmingham in 1957, he came because he wanted to see Fred Shuttlesworth. I had the privilege to meet the President and Fred Shuttlesworth at the Birmingham Union Terminal on a sidetrack in the yard and was photographed with them. President Truman told Fred Shuttlesworth, "You keep up your work. I am proud of you."

ORZELL BILLINGSLEY, attorney-at-law. I knew Orzell in the early 1950's and afterward. I remember when he graduated from law school in 1951 with honors. He maintained an office in the Masonic Temple Building downtown Birmingham. He was a leading attorney. He was also an activist in the early Civil Rights Movement. He felt the pain of the common man. He encouraged Blacks to register to vote. I am surprised he was not killed in those early days. He defended people who were arrested in the early days of the Civil Rights Movement. For those who had no money he would still take their case. He pioneered many causes that made millions for other people but small payment for him. He founded and was Mayor of

Roosevelt City, Alabama. He was also a judge. He never became a rich man in part because very few ever paid their legal fees. He was and is a treasured friend and advisor.

REV. ABRAHAM WOODS, present pastor of ST. JOSEPH BAPTIST CHURCH. He was a friend of my early youth. I feel that I have known him for most of my life. He is a soul winner and a Civil Rights leader. He helped pioneer the early Civil Rights Movement in Alabama. It has been my pleasure to visit in his church and to call his church my church when I am in Birmingham. He is also the leader of SCLC in Birmingham. He is one of the most enjoyable speakers of all time. In the early movement, the Alabama Christian Movement for Human Rights would meet on Monday nights in churches throughout Birmingham. Rev. Woods was the lookout after the meetings were over. He would always exit first to check if there were dangers lurking in the darkness.

DR. A. G. GASTON. I feel I have known Dr. Gaston all my life. He was the owner of Smith & Gaston Funeral homes in Alabama. He owned the Booker T. Washington Insurance Company, a radio station, WENN, in Birmingham, Alabama and many other business enterprises. He was a millionaire many times over, but he never forgot his early beginnings. He once offered me a million dollars when I was a young Bible student at Southeastern Bible College in Birmingham. Two other young Bible students and I were traveling in four states, Alabama, Georgia, Mississippi and Florida, to challenge people to register to vote. We were traveling in an old beat-up Cadillac automobile. Mr. Gaston said to me, "Weaver, I want you to get you a decent automobile." I replied, "Mr. Gaston, just give us your blessings." He did. Later I was glad that I took his blessing because the money would have been gone, but his blessing has lasted all these years. When he died I was privileged to be at his funeral and sit with the family. It was the biggest funeral the State of Alabama had ever seen. Governor Fob James spoke as did other notables. I counted over 50 limousines. The church and surrounding grounds were packed with people who came to pay tribute to this great man. When he died, he was over 100-years-old. I hope that Kelly-Ingram Park, where I played as a small boy while attending Henley Elementary School, will be re-named for A. G. Gaston.

ARTHUR SHORES, Attorney-at-Law and one of Birmingham's greatest attorneys. When I ran for Birmingham City Council, he gave me his support. I remember him as a young lawyer, he defended many civil rights activists. When the freedom riders came to Alabama and were arrested, he defended them. I remember when the KKK burned crosses on his front lawn. He will never be forgotten.

His secretary, Mrs. Agnes Stutermyer, always remembered my voice on the telephone. Even if I had not talked to her in years, I would call and she would always know me the moment I spoke. She was a dear person. She brought Ruby Hurley and me together.

MRS. RUBY HURLEY was a leader of the NAACP in Alabama before it was outlawed by the Alabama legislature. I met her in an office at the Masonic Temple in downtown Birmingham in the early 1950's. She was an inspiration. She said to me, "What's a White boy like you want to go and get yourself killed for?" She worked on after the NAACP was outlawed from Atlanta. She once told me that before 1955, there had been 6,000-plus lynchings in the southern sates of Alabama, Georgia, Mississippi, Florida, Tennessee and South Carolina. I can never forget her. I can honestly say I loved her like the sister that I never had.

REV. GEORGE PHIFFER. He was better known as praying Phiffer. Never in my life did I ever know a man who could bring the heavens down with a prayer. He told me after the mobbing at the Birmingham Union Railway Station, "Brother Weaver, we saw you over there and we couldn't help you. But I prayed for you." I have often thought his prayer probably saved my life that day. He left Birmingham and went to White Plains, New York.

DR. MARTIN LUTHER KING, JR. One of the greatest statesmen this world has ever seen. If he had lived, he could have been President. His marches in the Civil Rights Movement electrified the world. His death was a tragedy. I have visited his grave in Atlanta, Georgia many times. I only met him once in Montgomery, Alabama—just after he had accepted the call to become the pastor of the Dexter Avenue Baptist Church in 1953. I followed his career from beginning to end with

great respect and admiration. When the bill was before
the United States Senate to make a national Holiday in
his memory, Senator Jessie Helms led the fight in opposition. Many accusers called Dr. King a communist.
One was Senator Barry Goldwater. Almost immediately
during the debates a deal was cut between the King
family, the attorney general and the President to take
hundreds of documents that were thought to be nega-
tive and seal them in the archives until the year 2027.
This material was delivered to the custody of the
National Archives and Records Service to be maintained by the Archivist of the United States under a seal
for a period of 50 years. I always felt that the King family should have insisted that those charges be answered
at that time. I, too, was called a communist when I ran
for the Birmingham City Council against Eugene "Bull"
Connor. I never believed for one minute that there was
any truth to the charges against Martin Luther King, Jr.
I still believe that the King family should ask that these
sealed, archived documents be released immediately so
the American people can decide for themselves.

I want to say something about those persons who
would use JAMES EARL RAY for publicity purposes.
There are those who would gain publicity for themselves by seeking a new trial for him. In my opinion,
the man is scum, a confessed assassin, a convicted
felon, a fugitive, and a disgrace to the armed services
by his own admission. He shot Dr. Martin Luther
King, Jr. and fled. He dropped the rifle and his finger-
prints were found on the gun. He was later caught in
London, England. He was carrying false Canadian

passports trying to fly to Belgium. He later confessed to killing Dr. King before a court in Memphis, Tennessee and by a plea bargain, received life instead of death. He was 40-years-old and already on the FBI most-wanted list for escaping from a Missouri State Prison where he had been convicted for armed robbery. A native of Illinois, he had served previous sentences in California and Illinois, in the Federal Penitentiary and in Leavenworth, Kansas. He had been a drifter and was discharged from the Army for being a drug addict and for resisting arrest. He deserves no new trial and those who are pushing for it know it. However, there could be other people involved and they best look in that direction.

REV. VERNON JOHNS. His work inspired a movie—*The Vernon Johns Story*. He pastored the Dexter Avenue Baptist Church in Montgomery, Alabama 1950-1952. I believe he inspired the early bus boycotts. He was a great preacher. He motivated people to speak out and talk back. He inspired Afro-Americans to start their own businesses. After his death, his leadership and influence is still felt in the Civil Rights Movement. I met Rev. Johns in Montgomery, Alabama in 1951. He became my mentor. I still gain inspiration because of my early conversations with this great man. His motto was "Find a good fight and get in it."

In Greenwood Cemetery on Airport Road is located the tomb of JAMES POOLE, (June 17, 1888, died July 22, 1964). His wife is entombed there with him, LAURA BELLSER POOLE, (December 15, 1890 died October

14, 1962). The epitaph reads "They gave their today for our tomorrow." On the side of the tomb is another inscription. "He is of my right hand. I shall not be moved for this reason. My heart is glad and my soul rejoices all over. My body will also rest secure for thou will not leave my soul in the abode of the dead nor permit the holy one to see corruption." On the other side of the tomb are the words "I am the resurrection and the life and he who believes in me even if he dies, he shall live and whosoever lives and believes in me shall never die." Then there is the inscription "Faith, Hope and Charity." I am sure I first met the Poole Family in the 1940's when I was a young ambulance driver in Birmingham for the Luquire Funeral Home. Little did I know at that time what an important part they would play in my life. When I started an ambulance service of my own, JAMES POOLE helped me secure a used hearse and converted it into an ambulance. He also gave me a cot to go in the vehicle. His sons, JOHN POOLE and ERNEST POOLE, and their wives were also an important part of my life. When I was mobbed at the Birmingham Union Railway Terminal in 1957 and was almost killed, it was JOHN and ERNEST POOLE who perhaps saved my life. I remember hiding out in the POOLE FUNERAL CHAPEL when the Klan was looking everywhere for me. I remember hiding in a casket and being saved from almost certain death by the Poole's and their employees. AUBRY BUSHELON, ALVERY THOMAS, ADDIE WHITE and others protected my life at the risk of losing theirs. When ERNEST POOLE died I was honored to be on the funeral program. MATERIA POOLE, ERNEST

POOLE's wife is still at the helm of the POOLE FUNERAL CHAPELS and remembers this experience. I hope when I die, my funeral might be at the Poole Funeral Chapel because Birmingham was where it all happened and where the Poole's played such an important part of my life.

Also in Greenwood Cemetery are three civil rights martyrs, killed by a mad bomber, when he bombed the 16th Street Baptist Church on Sunday morning, ADDIE MAE COLLINS, who was born April 18, 1949. The epitaph on her marker reads "She died so freedom might live."

Just a few feet away is the grave of CYNTHIA DIONNE WESLEY, who was born April 30, 1949 and who was also killed in the explosion of the 16th Street Baptist Church in Birmingham, Alabama on September 15, 1963.

About a hundred yards north of these stones in the same cemetery, is the stone of CAROL ROSAMOND ROBERTSON, who was born April 24, 1949. She was also killed in the explosion of the 16th Street Baptist Church in Birmingham, Alabama on September 15, 1963.

Of the four young ladies killed in the explosion three are buried in Greenwood. One is buried in Shadowlawn, a perpetual care cemetery located across town. CAROL DENISE MCNAIR was also killed September 15, 1963. At this writing a move is underway to transfer this child to Elmwood Cemetery.

September 15, 1963 is a day that is well remembered in Birmingham, Alabama. Not only in Birmingham, but across America and around the world. That was the day that four young children lost their lives when a bomb exploded in the 16th Street Baptist Church in Birmingham, Alabama. Carol Rosamond Robertson, Cynthia Dionne Wesley, Addie Mae Collins, and Carol Denise McNair were killed instantly that Sunday morning. They were choir members getting ready to sing in a special children's service. They were dressed in white. Carol Rosamond Roberts, Cynthia Dionne Wesley and Addie Mae Collins were each 14-years-of-age. Carol Denise McNair was 11-years-old.

The Rev. Abraham Woods, Pastor of St. Joseph Baptist Church said at that time, "It was an awful scene." It might be noted that the Civil Rights Movement had reached a low ebb at that point in time. As the news of the explosion and the killing of the four young girls in the 16th Street Baptist Church in Birmingham, Alabama was flashed across America, it brought great attention to the south and in the Civil Rights Movement, things began to happen. I have always thought that these four children perhaps were the greatest martyrs of all in the Civil Rights Movement. They paid the price. I have also thought over the years that Bill Chambliss, who was convicted of this crime and later died in the Penitentiary, was not alone. The investigators should have looked North. Perhaps near Atlanta. Perhaps in Marietta, Georgia for another bomber. I believe that the Alabama authorities have the names of prime suspects and others should be arrested and prosecuted for this awful crime. I have also felt that then Governor George Wallace fanned the fires of racial hatred. In my opinion, George Wallace was an egotistical idiot. Every time I think of him, I think of the scripture Deuteronomy 32:35; "Vengeance is mine." My mother used to say, and I believe it, "Bread thrown on the water always comes back."

Greenwood Cemetery is being restored today because of the relentless efforts by Birmingham's distinguished Mayor, the Honorable Richard Arrington, and the City Council, led by the Honorable Aldridge Gunn. They would have tourists from all over America who visit the Birmingham Civil Rights Institute daily. Tour buses also turn through the two cemeteries—Greenwood and Shadowlawn—to honor these four children who gave their lives in the early Civil Rights Movement.

I wanted to bring to light or make mention of so many of those who made sacrifices in those early days during the struggle for Human Rights in the South. I want to mention some people who I think were heroes. They certainly had a lot more to do with the movement than I did. They had great accomplishments. They made great sacrifices. Those men and women were pillars of the Civil Rights Movement in the early days in the South.

I call them unsung heroes and some of them have received some recognition, but there are those who have not. I want to mention their names. On March 25, 1931, events were unfolding in northwest Alabama, the news would be flashed across America and attention would be drawn to the South because of charges made by two young White girls. One was 21 and one was 17. They were hitching a ride from Chattanooga, Tennessee to Huntsville, Alabama on a freight train. The two girls made charges they were raped by nine Negroes. The ages of the Negroes were 12 to 19. They were called the Scottsboro Boys. Thousands of Whites filled the Scottsboro thoroughfares and the nine boys were to be lynched. They were quickly convicted by a local court and eight of them to die. All hope had been given up for these young Afro-Americans until out of nowhere came a young lawyer by the name of SAMUEL LEIBOWITZ who undertook their legal defense. That was in 1933. These boys had been spared electrocution by the United States Supreme Court. It looked as if they would be executed but Samuel Leibowitz, with his able defense and his great passion for human rights and for justice, saved these Afro-Americans from certain death. Although I was just a young boy then, the Scottsboro Boys' trial was the talk of Alabama and everywhere. I always felt that without the able defense of Samuel Leibowitz they would have been executed and, in my opinion, it would have been a lynching. So this man has to receive recognition for saving these Afro-American from certain death.

Another hero of the early Civil Rights Movement was REV. ROBERT LEWIS ALFORD. He was pastor of the Olivet Monumental Church in Birmingham. Rev. Alford was a great believer that we are all created equal. He loved everybody. He was a pillar in the early Civil Rights Movement. Rev. Alford went home to be with the Lord on Thursday, July 25, 1991. "Gone but not forgotten." There are many pastors who would not allow the Alabama Christian Movement for Human Rights to meet in their churches. Many said they were afraid. Rev. Alford's church was always open to those who would like to meet like the Alabama Christian Movement which was founded by Fred Shuttlesworth after the NAACP was outlawed in Alabama.

I would like to respectfully pay tribute to a man who I knew and respected tremendously in Atlanta, Georgia. He was pastor of the Ebenezer Baptist Church for a number of years. I speak of the REV. MARTIN LUTHER KING, SR., better known as DADDY KING. Daddy King was born December 19, 1899 and died November 11, 1994. When I visited his grave in a cemetery on Jonesboro Road in Atlanta, Georgia, I was moved by the epitaph on his tombstone—"I love every-body and I am still in business. I just moved upstairs." God perpetuates the memory of this great man and his contributions which are numerous in the early Civil Rights Movement in America. His wife lies beside him.

I want to make mention of one of the greatest persons to touch my life. I have met seven Presidents and many U.S. Senators, congressmen and governors, but I have never known a man who I had more respect for than the man I met early in Birmingham in my youth. We stayed in touch by birthday cards and telephone for years after I left Birmingham up until he died. His name is VIRGIL L. HARRIS. Virgil was president of the Protective Industrial Insurance Company in

Birmingham and owned a funeral home by the name of
Davenport and Harris. When I decided to run for public office in the mid-1950's, I asked Virgil if he would
help me. He became my campaign manager. I always
told him that I felt bad because he had more education,
was smarter, and had more knowledge in his little fin-
ger than I had in my whole body. Yet I was the candidate and he was the one standing on the sidelines
cheering me on. There is no doubt in my mind that if
Virgil Harris had been born White, he could have been
anything he wanted to be. He could have been
President, governor, senator or congressman because he
was a fantastic individual. Virgil took over my campaign. We knew at the time that running against Bull
Connor would not be easy. We found out later that it
was also not a very healthy thing to do. We put signs up
and made trips all over Birmingham. We talked to a lot
of people and were met with tremendous resistance
because Bull was a household name and an avid segregationist. Virgil collected money. He got money from A.
G. Gaston and every Black funeral director in the area,
as well as every Black insurance company. We bought
radio time and we put ads in the paper. I came out with
about 3500 votes. I ran third in a field of five, but I
never would have done that well if it had not been for
Virgil. Virgil came up with some tremendous ideas during the campaign. He came up with the idea of recycling which no one had ever heard of in those days. He
came up with no tax increase. He had so many brilliant
ideas that benefited my campaign. It was a real shame
that he was not the candidate. I will never forget his
efforts in the early Civil Rights Movement. He gave of

himself in so many worthy causes. People never knew the work and the contributions that Virgil Harris gave of his life and his family. I was always welcomed by Virgil and his wife in their home when I was mobbed at the Union Terminal in 1957 and when I had to go into hiding. Virgil and A. G. Gaston and others collected money so that I could go to Washington and testify before the first Civil Rights Committee of the U. S. Senate. Virgil perhaps was the man who influenced me most in the early Civil Rights Movement. I was motivated by Vernon Johns and Fred Shuttlesworth, but Virgil Harris was a man for all seasons. God, I loved that man. Virgil died September 3, 1988. He was born September 19, 1913. His earthly remains rest in Elmwood Cemetery. An unknown author once wrote a poem and I think he had Virgil Harris in mind when it was penned.

> *Do not stand at my grave and weep,*
> *I am not there,*
> *I do not sleep.*
> *I am a thousand winds that blow;*
> *I am the diamond glints on snow.*
> *I am the sunlight on ripened grain;*
> *I am the gentle autumn's rain.*
> *When you awaken in the morning's hush,*
> *I am the swift uplifting rush*
> *Of quiet birds in circled flight.*
> *I am the soft star that shines at night.*
> *Do not stand at my grave and cry.*
> *I am not there;*
> *I did not die."*

I have gone out many times to Elmwood Cemetery to visit his gravesite and I have sat and cried.

Another unsung hero is the REV. C. E. STEELE, pastor of the Bethel Baptist Church of Tallahassee, Florida. In those early days in the mid-50's when I wrote my book, "Violence in the South," Rev. Steele received several copies and distributed them. Rev. Steele was always there for me to offer advice and he had areas where I could go on weekends and talk to Black congregations. I always received help from Black funeral directors in the states of Florida, Mississippi, Alabama and Georgia. Rev. Steele was a great friend and one of the unsung heroes in the early Civil Rights Movement. I will never forget the night of June 19, 1957 in Crestview, Florida where I was visiting my mother and stepfather near Eglin Air Force Base where my stepfather was in the air force. We were all asleep and suddenly the screams of my mother woke us up. She yelled "Get up! Get up! The house is on fire!" and we ran through the house. We found the blaze was not from the house, but from my car which was parked in front. A huge cross was on the side of it and top of my convertible and the seats were ablaze. We got water and put it out. The KKK had found me and had done their work. We were beyond the city limits of Crestview, Florida. We could not get the fire department or the police to come. Later I was told that I was at the wrong place at the wrong time and to get out of town. Rev. Steele was of great help at that time.

On a recent visit to Birmingham I went to a cemetery in Trussville—the Jefferson Memorial Gardens East. I got there early in the morning. It was still dark and I drove into the cemetery and sat there for an hour or so waiting for daylight. When daylight came I walked into the cemetery and after an hour or so found the grave of Bull Connor. I sat down on the ground next to the grave and watched a beautiful sunrise and thought about Bull. I had known him a long time. I met Bull Connor in the early 40's when I was an ambulance driver and tried to get a license to drive for a local funeral home. I had a clash with Bull before the City Commission. I thought about Bull and how he was first elected to the City Commission in 1937, as I recall. He was an arch segregationist. I thought about Bull and the days that I lived in Birmingham and the days that I drove an ambulance as a young boy. "Segregation is what the people, want. Segregation is the best thing that we can have. We will never integrate." And everyone that knew Bull knew that he would make every effort to keep those promises. I know there are a lot of people that really hated Bull. Some despised him and thought he was evil. But as I looked at his grave, I wondered how anybody could hate a handful of clay. His stone read THEO EUGENE CONNOR 1917-1976. His wife is buried beside him. There must have been somewhere in the neighborhood of 40,000 Klan members in Birmingham in the area during the 1940's and 1950's. That number probably remained the same through out the 1960's, but I never heard of Bull saying that he belonged to the Klan. In fact, I heard him say many times that he did not belong to the Klan, but you would never know that by the way at times he seemed to cooperate with them and their actions. Bull wanted Blacks and Whites to live in separate neighborhoods. In fact, Birmingham had an ordinance at one time that required that. In 1955 and 1956 I opposed him as a candidate for the Birmingham City Council and came in third in a field of five. Some called Bull Connor a hot head. He was a member of the Alabama Delegation in 1948 to the Democratic National Convention and after much arguing and some said "fisticuffs," Bull took a group and walked out and he said he could not support a party that could support a strong Civil Rights platform. He claimed he was carrying out his pledge to the people of Alabama and told everybody good-bye. It is ironic that one of the men who stayed in the party in Philadelphia and who was considered a segregationist was George C. Wallace, who later became Governor of the state of Alabama.

I knew George Wallace. He did not like Blacks. In that respect, he and Bull Connor were two of a kind. Bull Connor had more class. Wallace would do anything to get you to notice him. He would do anything to get votes and was jealous of everyone around him. He had to be the star of the show. He was a womanizer, would not tell the truth and could not be trusted.

During my early days in the Civil Rights Movement in Birmingham, I did not clash with Bull Connor as much as Fred Shuttlesworth, a local minister. Fred and Bull were at it all of the time and even when I ran against Bull in 1955 and 1956, he often called me and said

"Weaver, I want you to get out of town and leave the state, because I do not want to see you get killed and please, will you take Fred Shuttlesworth with you?" Now, that was good advice and I did leave later in 1957.

Bull Connor served on the Alabama Public Service Commission. In my opinion, Bull could have been Governor of Alabama. He was well liked and was a popular politician of his day. People liked him because he vowed that the races would never mix in Alabama or in Birmingham. I stood at his grave and I prayed a prayer. "Lord, may his soul and all those departed to the mercy of God, may they rest in peace." I felt neither malice, nor hatred for Bull Connor. Eleanor Roosevelt once told me to thank God for Bull Connor, for if he had not loosed the dogs, the hoses, and showed so much bitterness towards those who were trying to march, then the Civil Rights movement might not have gotten off the ground. Mrs. Roosevelt said that when he did what he did, these unthinkable acts created awareness around the world for the Civil Rights Movement. The beating of people who came south on the buses and the killing of some of the Civil Rights workers in the South, as well as the bombing of the children at the 16th Street Baptist Church, caused the world to focus on Birmingham. Mrs. Roosevelt said this attracted public sympathy across the world and certainly this helped the efforts of the Civil Rights Movement and that we certainly would not have gained such ground in those early days had it not been for Bull Connor. I think she was right. One other note. The reason Bull Connor decided not to run in 1953 was an incident that had happened in December 1951. He was caught in the Tutwiler Hotel with his secretary Christine Brown and he was charged with violating a City Ordinance of occupying a hotel room with a member of the opposite sex other than one's spouse. He was found guilty and was sentenced to 180 days and ordered to pay a $100.00 fine, but it was appealed and the Alabama Supreme Court overturned the conviction but this made Bull decline to run again in 1953. I might note I had a good friend who was the prosecutor in that case—J. Edmund Odom—a young attorney whom I knew very well.

On 11th Avenue North, in Birmingham is Oak Hill Cemetery, one of Birmingham's oldest cemeteries. It is cared for by the City of Birmingham. Herein lies the body of LOUISA (LOU) C. WOOSTER. She was best known as a famous "madam" of early Birmingham. It is said that she arrived when the town was not over one-year-old. She wrote her memoirs, **The Autobiography of Magdalen (1911)** telling about the "scourge of '73" when a cholera epidemic almost destroyed Birmingham. Many people died. The city was so young that many people had no kin to nurse them and Lou opened her heart and her house to them. She fed and nursed sick Black and White citizens, prepared the dead for burial and became a legend of early Birmingham. It was not proper for a gentleman to attend her funeral, but dozens sent their drivers to it. Her coffin was followed up Nineteen Street hill by empty carriages. God bless her memory. Many notable, governors and famous statesmen are buried in this cemetery, but Lou is my favorite.

WILLIAM E SHORTRIDGE, born March 17, 1900, died April 18, 1964. Bill was a great friend. He was a Black funeral director in Ensley, a suburb of Birmingham. In the Civil Rights Movement, he became known as the "bag man." When workers would get in jail that had no money, he would garner the money and bail them out of jail. Pinkey Shortridge, his wife, was also a great Civil Rights activist.

JOSEPH B. WELCH, who was born February 4, 1893, died June 22, 1960, owned a Black funeral home on 8th Avenue North. It was an old ante-bellum residence that at one time had been a nursery. In the back yard, there was a sandbox and my young friend, David, and I would often play there. That's how I met PA WELCH. He became a great friend and when I was involved in the early Civil Rights Movement, he helped me in many ways. He once gave me a gun and said to me "Weaver, shoot the hell out of them if they crowd you." He took several hundreds of my book, **Violence in the South**, and sold them. He and his sisters ran a small insurance company.

ROBERTA ROLAND (1897-1955) was a friend of my mother's and an early nanny for me. She was a people person who was always taking them to the doctor. She had a radio program on the Black radio station. I have never forgotten her because she was good to me, kind and gentle always. She frequently told me "Lamar, you be good." I remember answering her reminders with , "Yes, Miss Roberta." I have visited her grave many times in New Grace Cemetery. She is buried there with two of her sisters. I loved her very much.

The REV. MAURICE MCCRACKIN (1905-1997) was a great activist. When I went to Cincinnati in 1957, he welcomed me with open arms. He opened the doors of his church to me and introduced me throughout the city. The Rev. McCrackin fought war, segregation and homelessness. The Rev. McCrackin led a life dedicated to social justice and spent many years living among the poor and dispossessed in Cincinnati, Ohio. He fought segregation every time its ugly head appeared. In 1990, he scaled the White House fence to protest the Gulf War. I was blessed every time I was near the man.

The REV. EDWARD GARDNER, pastor and Civil Rights leader was always there to support all in the early movement.

EARNEST BROMLEY of Cincinnati, Ohio, was a war resister and one of the original freedom riders who spoke out against racial segregation in the South. I was privileged to be his friend.

THOMAS J. GARDNER, a friend for many years. He was related to A. G. Gaston and managed Smith & Gaston Funeral Homes in Birmingham. He invited me as a young student from Southeastern Bible College to speak to the employees of the funeral home and the insurance company which Mr. Gaston owned. I spoke to this group in the chapel of the funeral home. This began a great and long friendship with the Gardner's and the Gaston's and perhaps was my inroads to the Civil Rights Movement.

T. J. LANE. My dear friend, Terry. He pastored a church in Birmingham on the south side and when I was running from the Klan, he allowed me to stay at his home for a few days. He left Birmingham and went to Cincinnati, Ohio to become pastor of the New Prospect Baptist Church. He shared his pulpit with me on many occasions. He was an early activist in the Civil Rights Movement.

REV. GEORGE SANGSTER, pastor of the Revelation Baptist Church in Cincinnati, Ohio. When I was fleeing the KKK, I stopped in Huntsville, Alabama to speak to a group at Alabama A.M.E. College. The KKK found out I was in Huntsville and attempted to ambush me, but a member of the college faculty whisked me to Decatur, Alabama, a few miles away. I caught the L&N Train and stayed on to the end of the line which was Cincinnati, Ohio. I was met at the railway station by Rev. Sangster and Rev. A. L. Bland. Rev. Sangster welcomed me into his home and I later joined his church where my letter remains today. I remember telling Rev. Sangster that if I ever wrote a book, I would acknowledge him.

I know that I shall forget some but DEMETRIOUS NEWTON, a member of the Alabama Legislature was my first attorney in Birmingham. He is now the City

Attorney of Birmingham. When I was a guest of Representative ERNEST JOHNSON and spoke a prayer before that body, Representative Newton and Representative Johnson made a brief statement of my exploits in the early Civil Rights Movement before the Legislature. I will never forget PETER HALL, noted Birmingham attorney and jurist.

REV. H. C. BOYD, Pastor of Albany Georgia's Shiloh Baptist Church. Rev. Boyd was the first pastor in Albany to have the courage to open his doors to the Freedom Riders who sought a place to assemble. He allowed the then, controversial SNCC worker Charles Sherrod to use a room in his church. This was during the height the church bombings in the south, especially in Alabama. Many of Albany's Black leadership had reacted strongly against the freedom riders. This was due to the tremendous amount of fear of reprisals by the Whites in the city.

RUEBEN JACKSON, a young man whom I have come to know and love. He was educated at Atlanta's Morehouse College. Rueben has a strong sense of commitment to justice and equality. He believes that Black people have an obligation to be as vigilant against injustices meted out by Blacks toward members of their own race as those perpetrated by Whites. He also believes that not enough emphasis has been placed on the contributions to the Civil Rights Movement that have been made by Whites and Jews. He believes that this has to change before any significant amount of resentment can be eliminated with this generation of young Blacks. They simply must be told the whole truth. He has helped with the editing and co-authoring of this book and who shows a deep insight and appreciation for the efforts of all unsung the heroes. Rueben's father-in-law is the Rev. H.C. Boyd mentioned above. Rueben Jackson's father, Rosco Jackson, was a pioneer entrepreneur from Jacksonville, Florida. Rosco Jackson, born in 1898, was the son of slaves and became one of the wealthiest Black men in the State of Florida.

To all of these and many, many more, I want to thank you for your friendship to me in those early days. I remember, because I was there.

About the Author

Lamar Weaver was born on January 11, 1928 in the Southern Town of Cassville, Georgia. Lamar Weaver has received numerous humanitarian awards for his work in the Civil Rights Movement and is honored in the Birmingham, Alabama Civil Rights Museum. He currently resides in Atlanta, Georgia.

www.ingramcontent.com/pod-product-compliance
Lightning Source LLC
Chambersburg PA
CBHW031238280526
45784CB00004B/1626